loneliness

loneliness

Edited by Charles Burke, FSC

Saint Mary's Press™

Genuine recycled paper with 10% post-consumer waste.
Printed with soy-based ink. 5090600

The publishing team included John M. Vitek, consulting editor; Brooke E. Saron, copy editor; Mary Koehler, permissions editor; Andy Palmer, designer and typesetter; Alan S. Hanson, prepress specialist; manufacturing coordinated by the production services department of Saint Mary's Press.

Printed in Canada

Printing: 9 8 7 6 5 4 3 2 1

Year: 2012 11 10 09 08 07 06 05 04

ISBN 0-88489-835-0

Library of Congress Cataloging-in-Publication Data

Loneliness / edited by Charles Burke, FSC.
  p. cm.
ISBN 0-88489-835-0
  1. Loneliness—Literary collections. I. Burke, Charles, 1935–
PN6071.L68L66 2004
808.8'0353—dc22

2004006216

Contents

Foreword

This work, *Loneliness,* was originally published by Saint Mary's College Press in 1970. The book was used in schools and parishes to inspire young people through contemporary words and pictures. The original edition has long been out of print, but we recently came across the work in our archives. This work, and its companion title, *Friendship,* immediately struck us as timeless classics.

The reflections in this work have stood the test of time; the truths within are applicable yet today. The words are thought provoking, meaningful, enduring, and lasting words of inspiration for young people whose hearts long for warmth and meaning. We made the decision to preserve the integrity of the original works from the 1970 edition; the language in most of the excerpts has been left in its original form. The design and photographs are new. The work represents a blending of timeless, classic words and modern images, bringing age-old wisdom to life with the aid of meaningful images to help the reader enter into deeper reflection.

We hope you enjoy this timeless classic as much as we have enjoyed bringing a fresh edition forward to aid young people in their search for human and Christian meaning.

John M. Vitek
President, Saint Mary's Press

Preface

Loneliness is a word that makes all of us feel uneasy. We hesitate to admit the deep fear we have of facing life alone, strengthened only by our individual self-confidence and personal faith in what we are about. The young search for warmth and security. Adolescents move cautiously out of the family into a world of their own—a place of challenges and uncertainties where group acceptance means so much and being left out fills one with an emptiness that is too painful for tears. Adults who have been fortunate enough to establish warm relationships of love and concern in their lives realize the constant risks that threaten them on every side—separations that ultimately force us all to face the reality of death itself.

But loneliness is not merely a negative experience. It can also be an opportunity for much growth and creative development. This book has been compiled with such a view in mind. Loneliness is a human experience that we must all face in our individual ways and in the circumstances that personally confront us, but we can find some valuable insights in the thoughts and experiences of those who have shared this same feeling of alienation before us. The readings and photographs in this book have been presented with the hope that, through thoughtful reflection, the reader may reach a more compassionate understanding of the subject.

Part I
Everyone Knows Loneliness

No matter what our age, most of us are familiar with the profound feeling of loneliness. It has haunted us from the dark nights of childhood when we awoke with a start and reached for a protective hand only to find that we were alone among the shadowy figures of our bedroom. Each of us has some experience of how it feels to be left out. Perhaps it was just a sandlot ballgame, maybe it was a special school dance, or it might have been something more serious—like the first time we understood the meaning behind the words, "your kind need not apply."

Being alone is the lot of every person born into this world. From the cutting of the umbilical cord at birth to the last breath at death, we are made more and more aware of what it means to be alone, to be autonomous individuals. It is one of our highest dignities and also one of our greatest burdens. We live in the tension of trying to fulfill our deep-seated need for relationship while maintaining our individuality—unity striving to harmonize with separateness. An awareness of this rhythm in life is essential if we are to learn the positive values of loneliness.

The selections on the following pages illustrate the inescapable role that loneliness plays in the life of each of us. Clark E. Moustakas offers us some especially good insights on this topic.

What I ask for is absurd: that life shall have a meaning.

What I strive for is impossible: that my life shall acquire a meaning.

I dare not believe, I do not see how I shall ever be able to believe: that I am not alone.

—Dag Hammarskjöld

The Isolated Man
Adapted from Clark E. Moustakas

Everyone is alone. Ultimately, each person exists in isolation. We face ourselves in silence, wending our way in our individual pathways, seeking companionship, reaching out to others. Forever, we move forward stretching to the skies, searching the realization of our inner nature. We map new meanings and perceive new patterns for old ways and habits. Alone, our life passes before us. Our philosophy, the meanings we attach to our work and our relations, each significant aspect of our being comes into view as new values are formed, as we resolve to bring human significance, to bring life to each new day, to each piece of work, to each creation.

In loneliness, every experience is alive and vivid and full of meaning. When we have been greatly isolated and restricted in movement, we deeply feel the value of openness, of freedom and expansiveness. Life takes on an exquisite meaning, an exhilarating richness. When we have lived in total darkness, we piercingly appreciate the sunlight, the fireside, the beacon, the beginning dawn. When we are cut off from human companionship, we discover a deep reverence for friendship, for the one who stands by in the hour of need and shame. In the days of pain and defeat, loneliness takes on a human depth. When we are sequestered from life, when we are purely alone and dying, when we are lost in a world of dreary emptiness, then color becomes exquisite, rich, desirable, fulfilling. When we have been sharply isolated and lonely, every moment is pure, every sound is delightful, every aspect of the universe takes on a value and meaning, an exquisite beauty. The isolated tree stretches out to meet its new neighbor; the lonely star twinkles and turns to face its emerging companions in the night; the lost child runs to loved ones with open arms.

Each of us has been alone and lonely, starved for companionship. Each of us has endured days or weeks of isolation. Then suddenly, miraculously, we greet each face with a radiance and warmth, with a spirit

of kinship, with a deeper and more genuine fellowship, in a totally different way than when we are constantly in the presence of others.

Every lonely person experiences deep joy and gladness, rapture and awe in the presence of a human voice, the quiet touch of a human hand, the ecstasy of simply standing face to face, or walking shoulder to shoulder with someone. Each person comes to recognize the richness of the blue sky, the white clouds, the brilliant colors of the rainbow, the glorious opening of a new flower; each item is born anew and takes on an entirely unique value. The lonely mountain climber, the isolated explorer, the pilot lost in the desert, the sailor adrift at sea—each has known the agony and despair of loneliness. Each has discovered with horrible starvation, disease, and unbearable freezing the growing terror of an untimely death. Each of us has searched within for a new meaning in life, a value in being alive, in breathing freely, in walking openly, in conversing with companions. In the face of final death, in isolation and loneliness, the discovery is made that life is rich in its resources and

its ways, that truth is universal, that wisdom and love and reverence are rooted in every living meeting, that each individual stretches forward to touch a universal humanity.

In time of abiding loneliness and suffering, the value and meaning of life are reexamined. People lost in the mountains, in the desert, at sea, people faced with slow, painful death, people craving food and water, begin to consider the past. They search for deeper meanings in life. They review their relations. They hear again the words of love and hate they have spoken, the individuals they have violated with criticisms, recriminations, and competitive victories. They relive the scenes of meanness, pettiness, and dishonesty. They feel again the attachments they have known, the tender and cooperative endeavors. Everything of import comes to mind. When we are isolated, we search for answers to life. We seek a better life. We wish to be reconciled to ourselves and others. We realize the necessity of turning to lofty ideals, of finding the good and the beautiful in life, the simple and the true. In these hours we are honest and direct in facing our conflicts and problems, and in questioning our values. We search for a genuine basis for living, a way of loving every human being, a way to a life in which each person is respected and valued, in which each man is encouraged to find himself or herself and his or her own quantum in life. When we are lost and lonely, we seek deliverance. We seek to be forgiven our trespasses. We yearn for one more chance to absolve our-selves and our misdeeds, to rectify our sins against others, to turn the misery we have created into joy and happiness. In the face of slow death, each of us, in our own way, turns to God.

The deepest experience the soul can know—the birth of a baby, the prolonged illness or death of a loved relative, the tortuous pain or the isolation of disease, the creation of a poem, a painting, a symphony, the grief of a fire, a flood, an accident each in its own way touches upon the roots of loneliness. In all these experiences we must perforce go alone.

—Clark E. Moustakas

Between me and the sunset, like a dome
Against the glory of a world on fire,
Now burned a sudden hill,
Bleak, round, and high, by flamelit height made higher
With nothing on it for the flame to kill
Save one who moved and was alone up there
To loom before the chaos and the glare
As if he were the last god going home
Unto his last desire.

Dark, marvelous, and inscrutable he moved on
Til down the fiery distance he was gone,
Like one of those eternal, remote things
That range across a man's imaginings
When a sure music fills him and he knows
What he may say thereafter to a few men,
The touch of ages having wrought
An echo and glimpse of what he thought
A phantom or a legend until then;
For whether lighted over ways that save,
Or lured from ail repose,
If he go on too far to find a grave,
Mostly alone he goes.

—Edwin Arlington Robinson

Part 2
The Need for Others

Before we were able to say the words, "Can I go with you?" we felt a deep need to be with others. It has never been easy to wave good-bye. As children we physically clung to our parents and depended on them for the simplest things in life. Even as we grew older, we learned that the deepest happiness was to be found in sharing ourselves and our experiences with others.

This sharing with others is not just a matter of physical support, although that is not something to be lightly overlooked. It is a deep-rooted need to share in the entire life of another human being. We are drawn to share in the most profound aspects of one another's lives in an effort to share in the meaning of life itself. This ideal love relationship has its beginning with our conception and culminates in the cosmic union of all people in death and what lies beyond. It is this development of love relationships that parallels our own quest for happiness.

The photos in this section portray the mutual love that is so dependent on others from the earliest days of childhood. Love speaks in many ways other than words, and the silent sharing of one another's presence is not the least among these.

When the child cannot obtain adult presence and participation, loneliness results. The child attempts to assuage the feeling of isolation by entering into a rich fantasy life, and by engaging in imaginary personifications. The greater the intensity of separation, the greater the development of his sense of social isolation and parental rejection.

—Clark E. Moustakas

Each of us, as we grow, experiences a
sense of separation as a natural challenge
to the development of individuality. This
sense of isolation is dramatically felt by
the child. Because of a child's inability to
take care of herself or himself in the all-
important functions, communication with
others is a matter of life and death. The
possibility of being abandoned or left
alone is the most serious threat to the
child's whole existence.

—Clark E. Moustakas

Happiness! It is useless to seek it elsewhere than in this warmth of human relations. Our sordid interests imprison us within their walls. Only a comrade can grasp us by the hand and haul us free.

And these human relations must be created. One must go through an apprenticeship to learn the job. Games and risk are a help here. When we exchange . . . handshakes, compete in races, join together to save one of us who is in trouble, cry aloud for help in the hour of danger only then do we learn that we are not alone on earth.

Each man must look for himself to teach him the meaning of life. It is not something discovered: it is something moulded. These prison walls that this age of trade has built up round us, we can break down. We can still run free, call to our comrades, and marvel to hear once more, in response to our call, the pathetic chant of the human voice.

—Antoine de Saint-Exupery

Every deed and every relationship is surrounded by an atmosphere of silence. Friendship needs no words—it is solitude delivered from the anguish of loneliness.

—Dag Hammarskjöld

Part 3
Loneliness Has Value

As much as we fear loneliness, we have probably been relieved more than once when we could be by ourselves and work out some pent-up emotions. "Just leave me alone" is a phrase that can express utter exasperation or deep hurt, but in either case it indicates some personal awareness that being alone has healing effects. Time for quiet reflection is treasured by anyone who leads an active life in the rough and tumble world of today. A day off here, an hour there, or even a few minutes during a quiet coffee break may be just enough to restore our equilibrium.

Sometimes we may be forced by unexpected separations to reevaluate our friends and loved ones. Sickness, war, and death have a way of forcing us to appreciate many things that we so often take for granted. Even periods away from those we love because of schooling or business give us food for reflection as we lie awake in the dorm during the early morning hours or stare out the window of a jet at 30,000 feet.

Clark E. Moustakas offers his own reflections on the value of loneliness in the following pages. His insight into the relationship between love and loneliness shows much perceptiveness and sensitivity.

The Value of Loneliness
Adapted from Clark E. Moustakas

To love is to be lonely. Every love eventually is broken by illness, separation, or death. The exquisite nature of love, the unique quality or dimension in its highest peak, is threatened by change and termination, and by the fact that the loved one does not always feel or know or understand. In the absence of the loved one, in solitude and loneliness, a new self emerges, in solitary thought. The loneliness quickens love and brings to it new perceptions and sensitivities, and new experiences of mutual depth and beauty.

All love leads to suffering. If we did not care for others in a deep and fundamental way, we would not experience grief when they are troubled or disturbed, when they face tragedy or misfortune, when they are ill and dying. Every person is ultimately confronted with the pain of separation or death, with tragic grief which can be healed in silence and isolation. When pain is accepted and felt as one's own, at the center of being, then suffering grows into compassion for other human beings and all living creatures. Through pain, the heart opens, and out of the sorrow come new sensations of levity and joy.

All suffering that is accepted and received with dignity eventuates in deepened sensitivity. We cannot be sensitive without knowing loneliness. To see is to be lonely—to hear, feel, touch—every vital, solitary experience of the senses is a lonely one. Anyone who senses with a wide range of delicate feelings and meanings experiences loneliness. To be open to life in an authentic sense is to be lonely, for in such openness one hears and feels and senses beyond the ordinary. Through loneliness we are refined and sensitized and open to life's lofty ideals and influences. We are enabled to grow in awareness, in understanding, in aesthetic capabilities, in human relations.

Loneliness has a quality of immediacy and depth, it is a significant experience—one of the few in modern life—in which we

commune with ourselves. And in such communion we come to grips with our own being. We discover life, who we are, what we really want, the meaning of our existence, the true nature of our relations with others. We see and realize for the first time truths that have been obscured for a long time. Our distortions suddenly become naked and transparent. We perceive ourselves and others with a clearer, more valid vision and understanding.

In absolutely solitary moments, we experience truth, beauty, nature, reverence, humanity. Loneliness enables us to return to a life with others with renewed hope and vitality, with a fuller dedication, with a deeper desire to come to a healthy resolution of problems and issues involving others, with possibility and hope for a rich, true life with others.

Loneliness keeps open the doors to an expanding life. In utter loneliness, we can find answers to living, we can find new values to live by, we can see a new path or direction. Something totally new is revealed.

In the dark, despairing hours, sometimes only through loneliness can we bear to return to confront ugly faces and listen to criticism, and experience hurts inflicted by those we love most. When we have felt totally forlorn, desolate, and abandoned, we can arrive at a new depth of companionship and a new sense of joy and belonging. When we can leave ourselves to our own loneliness, we can return to ourselves with a new commitment to our fellow human beings. Not an escape from loneliness, or a plan, not strategy and resolution, but direct facing of our loneliness with courage, letting be all that in its fullness—this is a requirement of creative living. To be worthy of our loneliness is an ultimate challenge, a challenge which if realized, strengthens us and puts us more fully in touch with our own resources. At first, the experience of loneliness may be frightening, even terrifying, but as we submit to the pain and suffering and solitude, we actually reach ourselves, listen to the inner voice and experience a strange new confidence. We are restored to ourselves, and life again becomes meaningful and worthwhile.

The lonely sufferer helps himself or herself to a fuller realization of self, not by reducing his or her sense of pain and isolation, but by bringing its full extent and magnitude to consciousness. Great loneliness and suffering are met creatively, as potential growth experiences, only by surrendering to them, fully and completely. Salvation, self-growth, lies in giving full assent to loneliness and suffering, accepting what is, not fighting or resisting, not rationalizing or appealing to external helps, not demanding to know why we have been singled out for so much pain, but submitting ourselves to the experience in total self-surrender. Whoever is able to bear loneliness grows to the stature of his or her experience. Loneliness paves the way to healing, to true compassion, to intimate bonds with all living creatures and all aspects of nature and the universe.

The "never be lonely" theme is a reflection of the human estrangement from self in the world today. When we avoid facing directly a situation that contains the seeds of loneliness, we alienate ourselves from our own capacity for being lonely and from the possibility for fundamental social ties and empathy. It is not loneliness that separates us from others but the terror of loneliness and the constant effort to escape it. We must learn to care for our own loneliness and suffering and the loneliness and suffering of others, for within pain and isolation and loneliness we can find courage and hope and what is brave and lovely and true in life. Serving loneliness is a way to self-identity and to love, and faith in the wonder of living.

The moments between death and creation, the periods between the end and the beginning, the interval between completion and starting of a significant project are often times of deep loneliness. But in these intervals we can come to self-truths, to new strengths, and to new directions. Loneliness is often a painful and restless time. It leaves its traces in us, but these are marks of pathos, of weathering, which enhance dignity and maturity and beauty, and which open new possibilities for tenderness and love.

Loneliness is as much a reality of life as night and rain and thunder, and it can be lived creatively, as any other experience. So I say, let there be loneliness, for where there is loneliness there is also sensitivity, and where there is sensitivity, there is awareness and recognition and promise.

Being lonely and being related are dimensions of an organic whole, both necessary to the growth of individuality and to the deepening value and enrichment of friendship. Let there be loneliness, for where there is loneliness, there also is love, and where there is suffering, there also is joy.

Part 4

The Loneliness of Rejection

Not everyone finds loneliness to be an incentive for stimulating thought or quiet reflection on one's purpose in life. For some, loneliness is the empty feeling that throbs within after tasting the bitterness of rejection. For those who have loved and found no return of affection have given themselves to a cause only to be betrayed, or have not even been able to volunteer before they were passed over—for all of them, loneliness is very painful.

The theme of rejection is strong in many popular songs that fill the music charts across the country. The sounds of radios and CD players have become escapes for us all—the young with their rock ballads of broken-hearted lovers, the adults with their blues from the past, and even the elderly with their mood music recalling what might have been. Each of us has some very personal moments that we recall with a special twinge of emptiness.

The song lyrics and photos on the next few pages should stir up some sympathetic vibrations in us all. It is hoped that these will not return us to melancholy depression but instead lead us to a greater compassion for those we see suffering similar rejection in the competitive arena of life.

"I Am a Rock"

Simon and Garfunkel

A winter's day in a deep and dark
   December
I am alone gazing from my window
To the streets below on a freshly
   fallin' silent shroud of snow
I am a rock
I am an island.

I build walls, a fortress deep and
   mighty that none may penetrate
I have no need for friendship
Friendship causes pain
It's laughter and it's loving I disdain
I am a rock
I am an island.

Don't talk of love
Well I've heard the words before
It's sleeping in my memory
I won't disturb the slumber of feelings
   that have died
If I never loved, I never would have cried
I am a rock
I am an island.

I have my books and my poetry to
   protect me
I am shielded in my armor
Hiding in my room
Safe within my room
I touch no one and no one touches me
I am a rock
I am an island
And a rock feels no pain
And an island never cries.

"Yesterday's Rain"

Eustace B. Baker

Yesterday's rain brings tomorrow's pain
Fallin' round my head
The feeling I dread
Love has lost, you'll pay the cost
With a broken dream and still it seems
That I can't get out from under my cloud
And see the light of day
And yesterday's rain falls again and again
And makes me feel the word not real.

Yesterday came just to bring me misery
Till I can't see over my head
The darkness spreads into morning light
That turns into night
And all around me tears are falling
Like the birth of rain
And yesterday's rain falls again and again
And makes me feel the world not real.

Spinning to the ground
Hearing not a sound
Thoughts inside my head
Are going round and round
Got my mind on love
That I can never own
Friends all around me and I'm still all
  alone
Running through the trees
My hands above my head
Tryin' to escape the rain.

The darkness presses me against my pillow
While my ears ring with screaming memories
From every corner of my room.

God, I wish you were beside me!
Loneliness is not chased by half-empty beds
Nor by chucked-full days of people or words.

Sometimes I hold you sleeping,
Your head resting on my arm,
And my body melts warm and soft,
Floating on clouds of billowy-safe-closeness.

But awakening too often follows,
And once again I find loneliness my only bedfellow.

—Robert Cummins

She slumps against the window,
Passive, limp, lifeless,
But within, how she screams!
How she begs, soul outstretched,
for sanctuary.

—Deborah Florin

No man is an island, entire of itself; every man is a piece of the continent, a part of the main. If a clod be washed away by the sea, Europe is the less, as well as if a promontory were, as well as if a manor of thy friend's or of thine own were: any man's death diminishes me, because I am involved in mankind, and therefore never send to know for whom the bell tolls; it tolls for thee.

—John Donne

I exist as I am, that is enough,
If no other in the world be aware
   I sit content,
And if each and all be aware
   I sit content.

—Walt Whitman

Part 5

Loneliness Gives Insight

Sometimes the worst experience of our life later appears as the greatest stimulus to our success. Frequently environmental handicaps seem to cause opposite reactions in different people. Lack of affection in early childhood may lead one person to be very insecure and timid while another member of the same family might be quite aggressive. Poverty can force one individual to become depressed and dependent while another is stimulated to become resourceful and creative. Wealth has given birth to as many misers as it has philanthropists.

In a similar manner, loneliness may lead to either creative genius or suicide. The low points in our journey through life can become dark periods of despair. Our strength as individuals can often be measured by how we respond to being alone. If it is a traumatic experience for us to find ourselves home alone on a Saturday night, perhaps we have not yet learned to live with ourselves. Perhaps we fear that inner self we have so skillfully silenced over the years.

The selections on the following pages offer both positive and negative illustrations on the theme of loneliness. Personal reflection on the readings and photos found there will provide the reader with the opportunity to evaluate his or her attitude toward being alone.

Loneliness is a condition of existence that leads us to deeper reception, greater awareness and sensitivity, and insights into our own being. New images, symbols, and ideas spring from the lonely path. A person who lives his or her life accepting all significant dimensions of human existence is often a tragic person but a person who also loves life dearly. And out of the pain or loss, the bitter ecstasy of brief knowing and having, comes the glory of a single moment and the creation of a song for joy. In creative loneliness there is also a strange kind of relatedness—to nature and to other people—and through these experiences, a relatedness to life itself, to inspiration, wisdom, beauty, simplicity, value. We experience a sense of isolation and solitude, but we also maintain a relatedness to the universe. Only through fundamental relatedness can we develop our own identity. Our loneliness is an experience in growing that leads to differentiation of self. Our identity comes into relief as we breathe our own spirit into everything we touch, as we relate significantly and openly with others and with the universe.

Without any deep and growing roots in the soil of loneliness, we move in accordance with external signals. We do not know our place in the world, our position, where we are or who we are. We have lost touch with our own nature, our own spontaneity.

To the degree that we strive to attain a similarity or congruity, the degree that we act in order to be popular, to be victorious or to be approved of, we fail to emerge as a self, fail to develop our unique identity, fail to grow as a creative being consistent with our own desires and capacities and consistent with a life of genuine relatedness to others.

In actualizing our self, our aspirations, ideals, and interests, we often need to retreat from the world. We must have strength enough to withstand the temptations that arise when we are completely alone. This does not mean becoming uprooted or alienated. It means accepting the existential nature of our loneliness and seeing its value in the creation of being, in the emergence of self-identity, and in a more fundamental, genuine life. Cast in this light, loneliness becomes an illuminating experience, and it leads to greater heights.

—Clark E. Moustakas

. . . I knew what the loneliness of the long-distance runner running cross country felt like, realizing that as far as I was concerned this feeling was the only honesty and realness there was in the world and I knowing it would be no different ever, no matter what I felt at odd times, and no matter what anybody else tried to tell me. The runner behind me must have been a long way off because it was so quiet, and there was even less noise and movement than there had been at five o'clock of a frosty winter morning. It was hard to understand, and all I knew was that you had to run, run, run, without knowing why you were running, and on you went through fields you didn't understand and into woods that made you afraid, over hills without knowing you'd been up and down, and shooting across streams that would have cut the heart out of you had you fallen into them. And the winning post was no end to it, even though crowds might be cheering you in, because on you had to go before you got your breath back, and the only time you stopped really was when you tripped over a tree trunk and broke your neck or fell into a disused well and stayed dead in the darkness forever. So I thought: they aren't going to get me on this racing lark, this running and trying to win, this jog-trotting for a bit of blue ribbon, because it's not the way to go on at all, though they swear blind that it is. You should think about nobody and go your own way, not on a course marked out for you by people holding mugs of water and bottles of iodine in case you fall and cut yourself so that they can pick you up—even if you want to stay where you are—and get you moving again.

—Alan Sillitoe

Part 6

"All the Lonely People"

In 1966 the Beatles came out with a song that quickly found its way into the record collections of young and old alike. The loneliness of this woman named Eleanor Rigby struck a sympathetic chord across the nation and around the world. Its plaintive refrain, "All the lonely people, where do they all come from" echoed the personal experiences of millions. The futility of life has been felt by everyone at some time or another, and the loneliness of unfulfilled love and unappreciated service has haunted many more than just Eleanor Rigby and Father McKenzie.

Certainly there are numerous middle-aged women who feel a loneliness that is unique to unfulfilled love. But there are also those younger men and women who experience the sadder emptiness of never having found anyone or anything that caught fire in their hearts and gave them something to live for. Nothing is more depressing than the sight of a person who has never heard the voice of that inner god called enthusiasm. The individual who seeks meaning and happiness in a dream world of cult or escapism is condemned to lonely drifting from one high to another.

The mood for this section is set by the lyrics of the song "Eleanor Rigby" and is concluded by the final line of the poem "Miniver Cheevy." A haunting effect of questioning futility pervades the photos and literary selections and makes it difficult to escape the question: "All the lonely people, where do they all come from?"

"Eleanor Rigby"

John Lennon and Paul McCartney

Ah, look at all the lonely people
Eleanor Rigby picks up the rice in the
 church
Where a wedding has been
Lives in a dream
Waits at the window, wearing the face
 that she keeps in a jar by the door
Who is it for?

All the lonely people, where do they all
 come from?
All the lonely people, where do they all
 belong?

Father McKenzie, writing the words of a
 sermon that no one will hear
No one comes near
Look at him working, darning his socks in
 the night
When there's nobody there
What does he care.

All the lonely people, ah, look at all the
 lonely people.

Rigby died in the church and was buried
 along with her name
Nobody came
Father McKenzie, wiping the dirt from his
 hands as he walks from the grave.
No one was saved.

All the lonely people, where do they all
 come from?
All the lonely people, where do they all
 belong?

Too tired for company,
You seek a solitude
You are too tired to fill.

—Dag Hammarskjöld

What makes loneliness and anguish
It's not that I have no one to share my
    burden,
But this:
I have only my own burden to bear.

—Dag Hammarskjöld

We go through life each day and night
Searching for someone
   Who will share our joys,
   Our fun and bliss,
   Our pain and sorrow.

But most search in vain,
For soon we want too much,
Too much from him . . .

At times you'll cry at night
For want of love,
A love you'll never find.

—Robert Cummins

I can't tell you why, he says one night to a friend. It's just every time I start an affair, I know how it's going to end. The end of everything is in the beginnings for me. It's going through the motions.

—Norman Mailer

"Miniver Cheevy"

Edwin Arlington Robinson

Miniver Cheevy, child of scorn,
 Grew lean while he assailed the seasons;
He wept that he was ever born,
 And he had reasons.

Miniver loved the days of old
 When swords were bright and steeds were prancing;
The vision of a warrior bold,
 Would set him dancing.

Miniver sighed, for what was not,
 And dreamed and rested from his labors;
He dreamed of Thebes and Camelot
 And Priam's neighbors.

Miniver mourned the ripe renown,
 That made so many names so fragrant;
He mourned Romance, now on the town
 And Art, a vagrant.

Miniver loved the Medici,
  Albeit he had never seen one;
He would have sinned incessantly,
  Could he have been one.

Miniver cursed the commonplace
  And eyed a khaki suit with loathing;
He missed the medieval grace
  Of iron clothing.

Miniver scorned the gold he sought,
  But sore annoyed was he without it;
Miniver thought, and thought, and thought,
  And thought about it.

Miniver Cheevy, born too late,
  Scratched his head and kept on thinking;
Miniver coughed, and called it fate,
  And kept on drinking.

Part 7
Lonely and Misunderstood

It's rather easy to condemn the derelicts that shuffle through our parks and warm themselves in public libraries and railway stations. The alcoholics of skid row and the addicts walking the streets are pitied or feared but seldom understood. The loneliness that haunts these people is beyond the imagination of most of us. We find it nearly impossible to grasp the defeat and bitterness that has gradually forced these men and women to play the role of outcasts in our society.

What is it that starts a person on the road to despair? A dozen failures, a loss of self-confidence, and then the nagging doubts of disbelief in everyone and everything? Or is it more often caused by someone else who loses patience, or fails to respond to expressions of love, or cannot believe in a "loser"? These are difficult questions for all of us to face, but we cannot always run away from the unpleasant situations in life.

The following pages give the reader an opportunity to give some serious thought to the question of misunderstood members of our seamy world. The short story "Uncle Ernest" could be told with hundreds of other names and places that each of us would be familiar with. Perhaps such a story can bring out a bit more understanding and compassion in us toward the lonely streetwalkers of our impersonal cities.

Down-hearted doubters dull and excluded,
Frivolous, sullen, moping, angry, affected,
    dishearten'd, atheistical,
I know every one of you,
I know the sea of torment, doubt, despair
    and unbelief.

—Walt Whitman

The anguish of loneliness brings blasts
from the storm center of death: only that
can be really yours which is another's, for
only what you have given, be it only in
the gratitude of acceptance, is salvaged
from the nothing which some day will
have been your life.

—Dag Hammarskjöld

"Uncle Ernest"

Alan Sillitoe

A middle-aged man wearing a dirty rain-coat, who badly needed a shave and looked as though he hadn't washed for a month, came out of a public lavatory with a cloth bag of tools folded beneath his arm. Standing for a moment on the edge of the pavement to adjust his cap—the cleanest thing about him—he looked casually to left and right and, when the flow of traffic had eased off, crossed the road. His name and trade were always spoken in one breath, even when the nature of his trade was not in question: Ernest Brown the upholsterer. Every night before returning to his lodgings he left the bag of tools for safety with a man who looked after the public lavatory near the town centre, for he felt there was a risk of them being lost or stolen should he take them back to his room, and if such a thing were to happen his living would be gone.

Chimes to the value of half past ten boomed from the Councilhouse clock. Over the theatre patches of blue sky held hard-won positions against autumnal clouds, and a treacherous wind lashed out its gusts, sending paper and cigarette packets cartwheeling along unswept gutters. Empty-bellied Ernest was ready for his breakfast, so walked through a café doorway, instinctively lowering his head as he did so, though the beams were a foot above his height.

The long spacious eating-place was almost full. Ernest usually arrived for his breakfast at nine o'clock, but having been paid ten pounds for re-covering a three-piece in a public house the day before, he had stationed himself in the Saloon Bar for the rest of the evening to drink jar after jar of beer, in a slow prolonged and concentrated way that lonely men have. As a result it had been difficult to drag himself from drugged and blissful sleep this morning. His face was pale and his eyes an unhealthy yellow: when he spoke only a few solitary teeth showed behind his lips.

Having passed through the half dozen noisy people standing about he found himself at the counter, all scarred and chipped haven for hands, like a littered invasion beach extending between two headlands of teaurns. The big fleshy brunette was busy, so he hastily scanned the list written out in large white letters on the wall behind. He made a timid gesture with his hand. "A cup of tea, please."

The brunette turned on him. Tea swilled from a huge brown spot—into a cup that had a crack emerging like a hair above the layer of milk—and a spoon clinked after it into the steam. "Anything else?"

He spoke up hesitantly. "Tomatoes on toast as well." Picking up the plate pushed over to him he moved slowly backwards out of crowd, then turned and walked towards a vacant corner table.

A steamy appetizing smell from the plate: he took up the knife and fork and, with the sharp action of a craftsman, cut off a corner of the toast and tomato and raised it slowly to his mouth, eating with relish and hardly noticing people sitting roundabout. Each wield of his knife and fork, each geometrical cut of the slice of toast, each curve and twist of his lips joined in a complex and regular motion that gave him great satisfaction. He ate slowly, quietly and contentedly, aware only of himself and his body being warmed and made tolerable once more by food. The leisurely movement of spoon and cup and saucer made up the familiar noise of late breakfast in a crowded café, sounded like music flowing here and there in variations of rhythm.

For years he had eaten alone, but was not yet accustomed to loneliness. He could not get used to it, had only adapted himself to it temporarily in the hope that one day its spell would break. Ernest remembered little of his past, and life moved under him so that he hardly noticed its progress. There was no strong memory to entice him to what had gone by, except that of dead and dying men straggling barbed-wire between the trenches in the first world war. Two sentences had dominated his lips during the years that followed: "I should not be here in England. I should be dead with the rest of them in France." Time bereft him of these sentences, till only a dull wordless image remained.

People, he found, treated him as if he were a ghost, as if he were not made of flesh and blood—or so it seemed—and from then on he had lived alone. His wife left him—due to his too vile temper, it was said—and his brother went to other towns. Later he had thought to look them up, but decided against it: for even in this isolation only the will to go forward and accept more of it seemed worthwhile. He felt in a dim indefinite way that to go back and search out the slums and landmarks of his youth, old friends, the smells and sounds that beckoned him tangibly from better days, was a sort of death. He argued that it was best to leave them alone, because it seemed somehow probable that after death—whenever it came—he would meet all these things once again.

No pink scar marked his flesh from shell-shock and a jolted brain, and so what happened in the war warranted no pension book, and even to him the word "injury" never came into his mind. It was just that he did not care anymore: the wheel of the years had broken him, and so had made life tolerable. When the next war came his back was not burdened at first, and even the fines and days in prison that he was made to pay for being without Identity Card or Ration Book—or for giving them away with a glad heart to deserters—did not lift him from his tolerable brokenness. The nightmare hours of gunfire and exploding bombs revived a dull image long suppressed as he stared blankly at the cellar wall of his boarding house, and even threw into his mind the scattered words of two insane sentences. But, considering the time-scale his life was lived on, the war ended quickly, and again nothing mattered. He lived from hand to mouth, working cleverly at settees and sofas and chairs, caring about no one. When work was difficult to find and life was hard, he did not notice it very much, and now that he was prosperous and had enough money, he also detected little difference, spending what he earned on beer, and never once thinking that he needed a new coat or a solid pair of boots.

He lifted the last piece of toast and tomato from his plate, then felt dregs of tea moving against his teeth. When he had finished chewing he lit a cigarette and was once more aware of people sitting around him. It was eleven o'clock and the lowroofed café was slowly emptying, leaving only a dozen people inside. He knew that at one table they were talking about horse-racing and at another about war, but words only flowed into his ears and entered his mind at a low pitch of comprehension, leaving it calm and content as he vaguely contemplated the positions and patterns of tables about the room. There would be no work until two o'clock, so he intended sitting where he was until then. Yet a sudden embarrassment at having no food on the table to justify a prolonged occupation of it sent him to the counter for tea and cakes.

As he was being served two small girls came in. One sat at a table, but the second and elder stood at the counter. When he returned to his place he found the younger girl sitting there. He was confused and shy, but nevertheless sat down to drink tea and cut a cake into four pieces. The girl looked at him and continued to do so until the elder one came from the counter carrying two cups of steaming tea.

They sat talking and drinking, utterly oblivious of Ernest, who slowly felt their secretive, childish animation enter into himself. He glanced at them from time to time, feeling as if he should not be there, though when he looked at them he did so in a gentle way, with kind, full-smiling eyes. The elder girl, about twelve years old, was dressed in a brown coat that was too big for her, and though she was talking and laughing most of the time he noticed the paleness of her face and her large round eyes that he would have thought beautiful had he not detected the familiar type of vivacity that expressed neglect and want.

The smaller girl was less lively and merely smiled as she answered her sister with brief curt words. She drank her tea and warmed her hands at the same time without putting the cup down once until she had emptied it. Her thin red fingers curled around the cup as she stared into the leaves, and gradually the talk between them died down and they were silent,

leaving the field free for traffic that could be heard moving along the street outside, and for inside noises made by the brunette who washed cups and dishes ready for the rush that was expected at midday dinnertime.

Ernest was calculating how many yards of rexine would be needed to cover the job he was to do that afternoon, but when the younger girl began speaking he listened to her, hardly aware that he was doing so.

"If you've got any money I'd like a cake, our Alma."

"I haven't got any more money," the elder one replied impatiently.

"Yes you have, and I'd like a cake."

She was adamant, almost aggressive. "Then you'll have to want on, because I've only got tuppence."

"You can buy a cake with that," the young girl persisted, twining her fingers around the empty cup. "We don't need bus fares home because it ain't far to walk."

"We can't walk home: it might rain."

"No it won't."

"Well I want a cake as well, but I'm not walking all that way," the elder girl said conclusively, blocking any last gap that might remain in her defenses. The younger girl gave up and said nothing, looked emptily in front of her.

Ernest had finished eating and took out a cigarette, struck a match across the iron fastening of a table leg and, having inhaled deeply, allowed smoke to wander from his mouth. Like a gentle tide washing in under the moon, a line of water flowing inwards and covering the sand, a feeling of acute loneliness took hold of him, an agony that would not let him weep. The two girls sat before him wholly engrossed in themselves, still debating whether they should buy a cake, or whether they should ride home on a bus.

"But it'll be cold," reasoned the elder, "walking home."

"No it won't," the other said, but with no conviction in her words. The sound of their voices told him how lonely he was, each word feeding him with so much more loneliness that he felt utterly unhappy and empty.

Time went slowly: the minute hand of the clock seemed as if it were nailed immovably at one angle. The two girls looked at each other and did not notice him: he withdrew into himself and felt the emptiness of the world and wondered how he would spend all the days that seemed to stretch vacantly, like goods on a broken-down conveyor belt, before him. He tried to remember things that had happened and felt panic when he discovered a thirty-year vacuum. All he could see behind was a grey mist and all he could see before him was the same unpredictable fog that would hide nothing. He wanted to walk out of the café and find some activity so that he would henceforth be able to mark off the passage of his empty days, but he had no will to move. He heard someone crying so shook himself free of such thoughts and saw the younger girl with hands to her eyes, weeping. "What's the matter?" he asked tenderly, leaning across the table.

The elder girl replied for her, saying sternly: "Nothing. She's acting daft."

"But she must be crying for some reason. What is it?" Ernest persisted, quietly and soothingly, bending closer still towards her. "Tell me what's wrong." Then he remembered something. He drew it like a live thread from a mixture of reality and dream, hanging onto vague words that floated back into his mind. The girls' conversation came to him through an intricate process of recollection. "I'll get you something to eat," he ventured. "Can I?"

She unscrewed clenched fingers from her eyes and looked up, while the elder girl glared at him resentfully and said: "We don't want anything. We're going now."

"No, don't go," he cried. "You just sit down and see what I'm going to get for you." He stood up and walked to the counter, leaving them whispering to each other.

He came back with a plate of pastries and two cups of tea, which he set before the girls, who looked on in silence. The younger was smiling now. Her round eager eyes were fascinated, yet followed each movement of his hands with some apprehension. Though still hostile the elder girl was gradually subdued by the confidently working actions of his hands, by caressing words and the kindness that showed in his face. He was wholly absorbed in doing good and, at the same time, fighting the feeling of loneliness that he still remembered, but only as a nightmare is remembered.

The two children fell under his spell, began to eat cakes and sip the tea. They glanced at each other, and then at Ernest as he sat before them smoking a cigarette. The café was still almost empty, and the few people eating were so absorbed in themselves, or were in so much of a hurry to eat their food and get out that they took little notice of the small company in the corner. Now that the atmosphere between himself and the two girls had grown more friendly Ernest began to talk to them. "Do you go to school?" he asked.

The elder girl automatically assumed control and answered his questions. "Yes, but today we had to come down town on an errand for our mam."

"Does your mother go out to work, then?"

"Yes," she informed him. "All day."

Ernest was encouraged. "And does she cook your dinners?"

She obliged him with another answer. "Not until night."

"What about your father?" he went on.

"He's dead," said the smaller girl, her mouth filled with food, daring to speak outright for the first time. Her sister looked at her with disapproval, making it plain that she had said the wrong thing and that she should only speak under guidance.

"Are you going to school then this afternoon?" Ernest resumed.

"Yes," the spokesman said.

He smiled at her continued hard control. "And what's your name then?"

"Alma," she told him, "and hers is Joan." She indicated the smaller girl with a slight nod of the head.

"Are you often hungry?"

She stopped eating and glanced at him, uncertain how to answer. "No, not much," she told him non-committally, busily eating a second pastry.

"But you were today?"

"Yes," she said, casting away diplomacy like the crumpled cake paper she let fall to the floor.

He said nothing for a few moments, sitting with knuckles pressed to his lips. "Well, look"—he began suddenly talking again—"I come in here every day for my dinner, just about half past twelve, and if ever you're feeling hungry, come down and see me."

They agreed to this, accepted sixpence for their bus fares home, thanked him very much, and said good-bye.

During the following weeks they came to see him almost every day. Sometimes, when he had little money, he filled his empty stomach with a cup of tea while Alma and Joan satisfied themselves on five shillings'-worth of more solid food. But he was happy and gained immense satisfaction from seeing them bending hungrily over eggs, bacon and pastries, and he was so smoothed at last into a feeling of having something to live for that he hardly remembered the lonely days when his only hope of being able to talk to someone was by going into a public house to get drunk. He was happy now because he had his little "girls" to look after, as he came to call them.

He began spending all his money to buy them presents, so that he was often in debt at his lodgings. He still did not buy any clothes, for whereas in the past his money had been swilled away on beer, now it was spent on presents and food for the girls, and he went on wearing the same old dirty mackintosh and was still without a collar to his shirt; even his cap was no longer clean.

Every day, straight out of school, Alma and Joan ran to catch a bus for the town centre and, a few minutes later, smiling and out of breath, walked into the café where Ernest was waiting. As days and weeks passed, and as Alma noticed how much Ernest depended on them for company, how happy he was to see them, and how obviously miserable when they did not come for a day—which was rare now—she began to demand more and more presents, more food, more money, but only in a particularly naive and childish way, so that Ernest, in his oblivious contentment, did not notice it.

But certain customers of the café who came in every day could not help but see how the girls asked him to buy them this and that, and how he always gave in with a nature too good to be decently true, and without the least sign of realizing what was really happening. He would never dream to question their demands, for to him, these two girls whom he looked upon almost as his own daughters were the only people he had to love.

Ernest, about to begin eating, noticed two smartly dressed men sitting at a table a few yards away. They sat in the same place the previous day, and also the day before that, but he thought no more about it because Joan and Alma came in and walked quickly across to his table.

"Hello, Uncle Ernest!" they said brightly. "What can we have for dinner?" Alma looked across at the chalk written list on the wall to read what dishes were available.

His face changed from the blank preoccupation of eating, and a smile of happiness infused his cheeks, eyes, and the curve of his lips. "Whatever you like," he answered.

"But what have they got?" Alma demanded crossly. "I can't read their scrawl."

"Go up to the counter and ask for a dinner," he advised with a laugh.

"Will you give me some money then?" she asked, her hand out. Joan stood by without speaking, lacking Alma's confidence, her face timid, and nervous because she did not yet understand this regular transaction of money between Ernest and themselves, being afraid that one day they would stand there waiting for money and Ernest would quite naturally look surprised and say there was nothing for them.

He had just finished repairing an antique three-piece and had been paid that morning, so Alma took five shillings and they went to the counter for a meal. While they were waiting to be served the two well-dressed men who had been watching Ernest for the last few days stood up and walked over to him.

Only one of them spoke; the other held his silence and looked on. "Are those two girls your daughters, or any relation to you?" the first asked, nodding towards the counter.

Ernest looked up and smiled. "No," he explained in a mild voice, "they're just friends of mine, why?"

The man's eyes were hard, and he spoke clearly. "What kind of friends?"

"Just friends. Why? Who are you?" He shuddered, feeling a kind of halfguilt growing inside him for a half-imagined reason that he hoped wasn't true.

"Never mind who we are. I just want you to answer my question."

Ernest raised his voice slightly, yet did not dare to look into the man's arrogant eyes. "Why?" he cried. "What's it got to do with you? Why are you asking questions like this?"

"We're from the police station," the man remarked dryly, "and we've had complaints that you're giving these little girls money and leading them the wrong way!"

Ernest wanted to laugh, but only from misery. Yet he did not want to laugh in case he should annoy the two detectives. He started to talk: "But . . . but . . ."— then found himself unable to go on. There was much that he wanted to say, yet he could enunciate nothing, and a bewildered animal stare moved slowly into his eyes.

"Look," the man said emphatically, "we don't want any of your 'buts.' We've known you for years in fact, and we're asking you to leave those girls alone and have nothing more to do with them. Men like you shouldn't give money to little girls. You should know what you're doing, and have more sense."

Ernest protested loudly at last. "I tell you they're friends of mine. I mean no harm. I look after them and give them presents just as I would daughters of my own. They're the only company I've got. In any case why shouldn't I look after them? Why should you take them away from me? Who do you think you are? Leave me alone . . . leave me alone." His voice had risen to a weak scream of defiance, and the other people in the crowded café were looking around and staring at him, wondering what was the cause of the disturbance.

The two detectives acted quickly and competently, yet without apparent haste. One stood on each side of him, lifted him up, and walked him by the counter, out on to the street, squeezing his wrists tightly as they did so. As Ernest passed the counter he saw the girls holding their plates, looking in fear and wonder at him being walked out.

They took him to the end of the street, and stood there for a few seconds talking to him, still keeping hold of his wrists and pressing their fingers hard into them.

"Now look here, we don't want any more trouble from you, but if ever we see you near those girls again, you'll find yourself up before a magistrate." The tone of finality in his voice possessed a physical force that pushed Ernest to the brink of sanity.

He stood speechless. He wanted to say so many things, but the words would not come to his lips. They quivered helplessly with shame and hatred, and so were incapable of making words. "We're asking you in a peaceful manner," the detective went on, "to leave them alone. Understand?"

"Yes," Ernest was forced to answer.

"Right. Go on then. And we don't want to see you with those girls again."

He was only aware of the earth sliding away from under his feet, and a wave of panic crashing into his mind, and he felt the unbearable and familiar emptiness that flowed outwards from a tiny and unknowable point inside him. Then he was filled with hatred for everything, then intense pity for all the movement that was going on around him, and finally even more intense pity for himself. He wanted to cry but could not: he could only walk away from his shame.

Then he began to shed agony at each step. His bitterness eddied away and a feeling the depth of which he had never known before took its place. There was now more purpose in the motion of his footsteps as he went along the pavement through midday crowds. And it seemed to him that he did not care about anything any more as he pushed through the swing doors and walked into the crowded and noisy bar of a public house, his stare fixed by a beautiful heavily baited trap of beer pots that would take him into the one and only best kind of oblivion.

"A Most Peculiar Man"

Simon and Garfunkel

He was a most peculiar man.
That's what Mrs. Reardon said,
And she should know—
She lived upstairs from him.
She said he was a most peculiar man.

He was a most peculiar man.
He lived all alone,
Within a house, within a room,
Within himself.
A most peculiar man.

He had no friends
He seldom spoke.
And no one in turn
Ever spoke to him
'Cause he wasn't friendly
And he didn't care
They said he was a most peculiar man.

He died last Saturday.
He turned on the gas
And he went to sleep
With the windows closed
So he'd never wake up
To his silent word
And his tiny room.
And Mrs. Reardon says
He has a brother somewhere
Who should be notified soon.
And all the people said:
What a shame that he's dead,
But wasn't he a most peculiar man.

"Richard Cory"

Edwin Arlington Robinson

Whenever Richard Cory went down
town,
We people on the pavement looked at
him:
He was a gentleman from sole to crown,
Clean favored, and imperially slim.

And he was always quietly arrayed,
And he was always human when he
talked;
But still he fluttered pulses when he said,
"Good-morning," and he glittered when
he walked.

And he was rich—yes, richer than a
king—
And admirably schooled in every grace:
In fine, we thought that he was everything
To make us wish that we were in his
place.

So on we worked, and waited for the
light,
And went without the meat, and cursed
the bread;
And Richard Cory, one calm summer
night,
Went home and put a bullet through his
head.

Part 8
I Am Not Alone

Loneliness is a paradoxical thing that can either force us to withdraw from those around us and turn in upon ourselves, or it can be the stimulus for reevaluation and greater sharing. The moments we spend alone, idly staring into space wondering about the why's and wherefore's of life, may be the most important moments of our lives. Personal convictions are often confirmed in such instances. The mystery of life becomes a bit more liveable as one or two pieces of the puzzle link together to add greater clarity to the picture.

Few men have had the opportunity to be as totally alone as Admiral Byrd was dur-ing his exploration of the South Pole. Cut off from all living creatures for several months in the Antarctic winter, Byrd learned what the limits of loneliness can mean for a person. When he felt that he was about to die from carbonmonoxide poisoning, he spent his last few ounces of energy writing down what he found most important about his experience of living alone in that frozen wasteland. His com-ments form the core of this final section.

The concluding remark by Dag Hammarskjöld is most appropriate. It states in a few words the entire thrust of this book.

He is one of those who has had the
wilderness for a pillow, and called a star
his brother. Alone. But loneliness can be a
communion.

—Dag Hammarskjöld

About 3 o'clock on the morning of June 2, I had another lucid phase. I tried without success to force my body into sleep. The sleeping pills were on the shelf. The flashlight fingered the bottle. I took it down and dumped the pellets into my cupped palm. There were more than two dozen, white and round; they bespoke a lovely promise. I reached for the bottle. But then I stopped. It was impossible to go on like this. I should become a madman, shrinking from every shadow and touch of pain. I found a match and lighted a candle. An unused sheet of paper lay on the bunk, on top of the diary. I wrote:

The universe is not dead. Therefore, there is an Intelligence there, and it is all pervading. At least one purpose, possibly the major purpose, of that Intelligence is the achievement of universal harmony.

Striving in the right direction for Peace (Harmony), therefore, as well as the achievement of it, is the result of accord with that Intelligence.

It is desirable to effect that accord.

The human race, then, is not alone in the universe. Though I am cut off from human beings, *I* am not alone.

For untold ages man has felt an awareness of that Intelligence. Belief in it is the one point where all religions agree. It has been called by many names. Many call it God.

—Richard E. Byrd

Pray that your loneliness
may spur you into finding
something to live for,
great enough to die for.

—**Dag Hammarskjöld**

Acknowledgments

The selections by Dag Hammarskjöld on pages 10, 27, 58, 59, 71, 97, and 100 are from his book *Markings,* translated by W. H. Auden and Leif Solberg. Copyright © 1964 by Alfred A. Knopf, a division of Random House, Inc., and Faber and Faber Ltd. Used by permission of Alfred A. Knopf, a division of Random House, Inc.

The selections by Clark E. Moustakas on pages 12–15, 17, 22, 23, 30–35, and 51 are adapted from his book *Loneliness and Love* (Englewood Cliffs, NJ: Prentice-Hall, Inc., 1972). Copyright © 1972 by Clark E. Moustakas. Reprinted with permission of Simon & Schuster Adult Publishing Group.

The selection by Edwin Arlington Robinson on page 18 is from his poem "Man Against the Sky," in his book *The Man Against the Sky: A Book of Poems.* (New York: Macmillan, 1916).

The selection by Antoine de Saint-Exupery on page 24 is from his book *Wind, Sand and Stars* (New York: Harcourt Brace Jovanich, 1939), pages 32–33. Copyright © 1939 by Antoine de Saint-Exupery, renewed in 1967 by Lewis Galantiere. Reprinted with permission of Harcourt, Inc.

The lyrics from the songs "I Am a Rock" and "A Most Peculiar Man" on pages 38 and 91, respectively, are by Paul Simon. Copyright © 1965 by Paul Simon. Use with permission of Paul Simon Music.

The lyrics from the song "Yesterday's Rain" on page 40 are by Eustace B. Baker. Copyright © 1968 by Ridge Music Corporation. Used with permission of Ridge Music Corporation.

The selections by Robert Cummins on pages 42 and 60 are from the original edition of *Loneliness*, edited by Charles Burke (Winona, MN: Saint Mary's College Press, 1971), pages 38 and 60. Copyright © 1971 by Saint Mary's College Press.

The selection by John Donne on page 45 is from "No Man Is an Island," in *Devotions Upon Emergent Occasions: Meditation XVII*, by John Donne, London 1624.

The selections by Walt Whitman on pages 47 and 70 are from his book *Leaves of Grass*. Copyright © 1944 by Doubleday and George H. Doran & Company.

Photo Credits